Reading Response Forms

Grades 1-3

Written by Margot Southall

Illustrated by S&S Learning Materials

ISBN 1-55035-382-2

Reading Response Forms, SSN1-165

Copyright 1998 S&S Learning Materials

Revised Feb. 2003

15 Dairy Avenue

Napanee, Ontario

K7R 1M4

All Rights Reserved * Printed in Canada

A Division of the Solski Group

Published in Canada by:
S&S Learning Materials
15 Dairy Avenue
Napanee, Ontario
K7R 1M4
www.sslearning.com

Published in the United States by:
T4T Learning Materials
5 Columba Drive PMB 175
Niagara Falls, New York
14305
www.t4tlearning.com

© S&S Learning Materials 1 SSN1-165

Look For Other Language Units

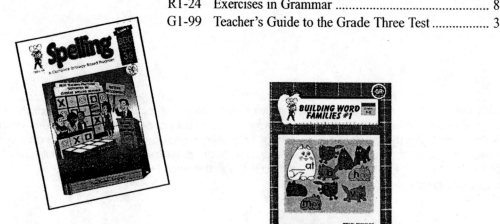

Published by:
S&S Learning Materials
15 Dairy Avenue
Napanee, Ontario
K7R 1M4

Distributed in U.S.A. by:
T4T Learning Materials
5 Columba Drive, Suite 175
Niagara Falls, New York
14305

© S&S Learning Materials

2

SSN1-165

Reading Response Forms

Table of Contents

Reading Response Forms

Teacher Planning Guide

1. Introducing the Reading Responses: First Session

- Select an appropriate reading response form for your grade level and the skill you wish to focus on (e.g. sequencing). Introduce the response form within a shared reading context, choosing a story that supports the skill, such as a circular story for sequencing.

- Present the reading response form to the class as an enlarged photocopy, or on the flipchart or blackboard. Read the instructions to the class and use a language experience approach to discuss and record the students' suggestions in completing the response. Be sure to restate the different suggestions of your students, in order to provide a range of alternative ways of responding to the activity.

- When the class model is completed you may ask students to complete their own responses to the shared reading or choose a different story and complete the response form based on that story.

2. Subsequent Sessions: Organization of the Responses

- Continue modeling each of the selected responses in a mini-lesson format. After several responses have been modeled, you may wish to distribute copies of these 3-5 responses in booklet form or in a duotang for students to practice their newly-acquired skills independently. By photocopying, sorting and collating a class/group set of copies for distribution, you may provide a focus for the reading sessions over the next week. The students may call these their Reading Response Logs.

Reading Response Forms

- When students have had sufficient practice on these responses, introduce another set one at a time and repeat the process, now distributing a set of 6-10 (previous + new set) to provide approximately two weeks of reading sessions. When selecting the responses, you may wish to alternate written and creative responses, as well as sequence them in order of difficulty.

- Maintain student motivation by adding and deleting specific activities in subsequent sets of responses. This enables a continuous introduction of new skills and practice sessions.

3. Mini-Lesson Options

- You may choose to concentrate on specific skill categories with a block of related responses or a selection from different skill areas. To extend student understanding of a particular story or novel, choose a response from each category to provide a comprehensive study which integrates a number of skills.

4. Sharing Reading Responses

- It is important to provide time for students to share their responses on a regular basis. For example, they may choose their favorite one to present to the class or group each week. In this way, designated students are sharing each day. If sharing is done in a group format there could be a daily sharing at the end of each reading session. Primary students need to verbally discuss and describe their responses to develop their comprehension skills. This also provides a model for other students. These "book talks" are a great source of motivation, as students describe and recommend classroom reading materials to their peers.

Reading Response Forms

5. Rotating Reading Groups

- Providing the class with sets of reading responses allows the teacher to work with small groups of students in guided reading sessions and on a one-to-one basis with students experiencing difficulty, while conducting reading assessments. You may wish to have different groups of students working on specific skill areas by completing related reading responses. They may then share these with the class and provide a model for other group skill sessions. This would be an effective way of approaching group story/novel stories.

6. Literary Suggestions

- Certain types of literature lend themselves to specific responses. For example, the character analysis and sequencing and summarizing activities are particularly suited to fairy tales, stories with a moral and novel studies. You may wish students to complete a response for each chapter of a novel, such as *James and the Giant Peach* by Roald Dahl. Stories with cumulative or circular patterns are also suitable for sequencing and summarizing activities. The vocabulary, creative, and synthesis and evaluation responses are applicable to a number of different types of literature.

7. Tracking, Assessment and Individual Programing

- The reading response tracking sheet provides the teacher with a record of the skill areas addressed in their program and completed by specific students. The student may wish to choose a completed response from each category and place this in his or her reading portfolio. The teacher may also refer to this compilation (reading response log) in assessing student comprehension and related reading skills.

Reading Response Forms

- Reading conferences and observation during "book talks" are also excellent opportunities for ongoing performance-based assessment. During a reading conference the student may use the response form as a reference to orally retell and comment on the story. The teacher may then question the student on the characters, plot, setting and author's message or purpose.

- Once the whole class is participating in the reading response program, there will be opportunities for individual assessment and appropriate programing through additional practice in areas causing difficulty. For example, a student experiencing difficulty sequencing the events of a story in logical order would be provided with additional modeling and practice of the responses addressing this need. In this way, classroom grouping may be organized with students with similar needs working together on specific reading responses. You may wish to have reading buddies from within your classroom or older students assist students with their reading responses.

8. Use of the Blank Form

- The blank form may be programed by the teacher to meet the individual needs of the classroom. You may wish to create some of your own forms to use with specific novels or stories.

Reading Response Tracking Sheet

Name: _____

Put a check mark in the box of each completed activity.

Vocabulary Development

- ☐ 1. People, Places, Animals and Things
- ☐ 2. Word Pictures
- ☐ 3. Action Words
- ☐ 4. Rebus Story
- ☐ 5. Words for *Said*
- ☐ 6. Story A B C
- ☐ 7. Word Scramble
- ☐ 8. Word Search
- ☐ 9. Interesting Words

Sequencing and Summarizing Events

- ☐ 1. Story Hamburger
- ☐ 2. Sum It Up!
- ☐ 3. Comic Strip
- ☐ 4. News Report
- ☐ 5. Story Map
- ☐ 6. Five W's
- ☐ 7. Story Countdown
- ☐ 8. Plot Line
- ☐ 9. Who, What, Where

Character Analysis

- ☐ 1. Character Web
- ☐ 2. Character Portrait
- ☐ 3. Clever Character
- ☐ 4. Wanted Poster
- ☐ 5. Pen Pal
- ☐ 6. Story Friend
- ☐ 7. Which Character?

Creative Thinking

- ☐ 1. Design a T-Shirt
- ☐ 2. Book Cover
- ☐ 3. Favorite Part
- ☐ 4. Design a Home
- ☐ 5. Put Yourself in the Story

Synthesis and Evaluation

- ☐ 1. Fact or Fiction
- ☐ 2. Writer's Secrets
- ☐ 3. Story Frame
- ☐ 4. Story Riddles
- ☐ 5. New Ending
- ☐ 6. Good or Bad?
- ☐ 7. Like or Did Not Like
- ☐ 8. Solve a Story Problem
- ☐ 9. Story Feelings

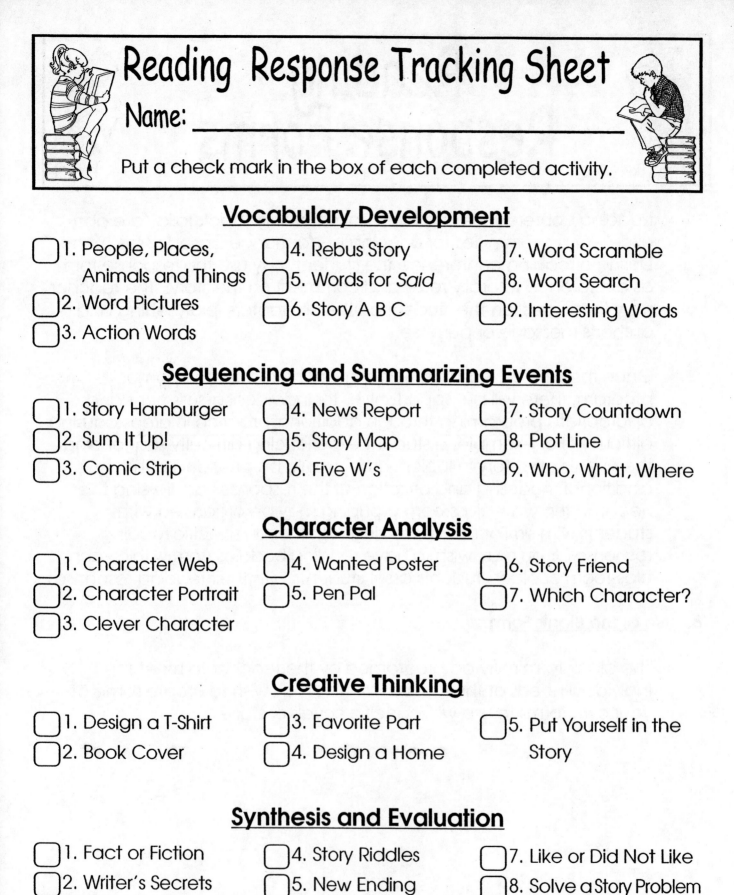

SSN1-165

Reading Response Forms

Reading Response Skill Categories

Vocabulary Development
1. People, Places, Animals and Things
2. Word Pictures
3. Action Words
4. Rebus Story
5. Words for *Said*
6. Story ABC
7. Word Scramble
8. Word Search
9. Interesting Words

Sequencing and Summarizing Events
1. Story Hamburger
2. Sum It Up!
3. Comic Strip
4. News Report
5. Story Map
6. Five W's
7. Story Countdown
8. Plot Line
9. Who, What, Where

Character Analysis
1. Character Web
2. Character Portrait
3. Clever Character
4. Wanted Poster
5. Pen Pal
6. Story Friend
7. Which Character?

Creative Thinking
1. Design a T-Shirt
2. Book Cover
3. Favorite Part
4. Design a Home
5. Put Yourself in the Story

Synthesis and Evaluation
1. Fact or Fiction?
2. Writer's Secrets
3. Story Frame
4. Story Riddles
5. New Ending
6. Good or Bad?
7. Liked, Did Not Like
8. Solve a Story Problem
9. Story Feelings

Reading Response Assessment

Name: _____

Circle a number from 1 to 4 to indicate the level achieved by the student.

Vocabulary Development:

- Demonstrates understanding of text at the word level. 1 2 3 4

- Locates and identifies specific word categories 1 2 3 4

Sequencing and Summarizing Events:

- Sequences events in correct order 1 2 3 4

- Summarizes main events in the story (plot) 1 2 3 4

Character Analysis:

- Describes personality traits of character 1 2 3 4

- Interprets role of character and supports with information from the text 1 2 3 4

Creative Thinking:

- Demonstrates appreciation of story content 1 2 3 4

- Represents the story in an artistic form 1 2 3 4

Synthesis and Evaluation:

- Makes generalizations and inferences based on own interpretation of the story 1 2 3 4

- Evaluates story elements and outcome 1 2 3 4

People, Animals, Places and Things

Name: _____

Title: _____

Author: _____

Vocabulary Development #1

Make a list of all the people, animals, places and things in your story.

e.g.

People & Animals	Places	Things
Sister Bear 	treehouse 	toys 

People & Animals	Places	Things
_____	_____	_____
_____	_____	_____
_____	_____	_____
_____	_____	_____
_____	_____	_____
_____	_____	_____
_____	_____	_____
_____	_____	_____

Word Pictures

Name: _____

Title: _____

Author: _____

Vocabulary Development #2

Find **four** things in your story. e.g.

Label each picture.

1. cat	2. house
3. tree	4. car

1.	2.
3.	4.

Action Words

Name: _____

Title: _____

Author: _____

Vocabulary Development #3

Action words tell what someone is doing.

e.g. **running, swimming, talking or drawing**

running

Copy **five** good action words from your story.

Draw a **picture** of one of your action words.

Print the word under the picture.

1. _____

2. _____

3. _____

4. _____

5. _____

Rebus Story

Name: _____

Title: _____

Author: _____

Vocabulary Development #4

A **rebus** uses pictures for some of the words.

Make a **rebus or picture story** of something that happened in your story.

e.g. The  was on the top of a  .

My Rebus Story

Words for *Said*

Name: _____

Title: _____

Author: _____

Vocabulary Development #5

When someone is talking in your story the author tells us who it is.

> e.g.   "She can play with my toys," **said** Sam.

The word **said** is used to tell us who is talking. Authors also use other words for *said*, such as **shouted**, **whispered** or **asked**.

Find **three** words that mean the same as *said* in your story.

Copy the sentence these words are in and put a line under the word that means the same as *said*.

1. _____

_____

2. _____

_____

3. _____

_____

Story ABC

Name: _____

Title: _____

Author: _____

Vocabulary Development #6

Find **ten** words in the story that begin with the same letter.

e.g. | boy, bat, ball, base |

ball

Print the words that you find.

Draw a picture of one of the words.

1. _____

2. _____

3. _____

4. _____

5. _____

6. _____

7. _____

8. _____

9. _____

10. _____

Word Scramble

Name: _____

Title: _____

Author: _____

Vocabulary Development #7

Choose **ten** words from the story. Make a **list** of your words in the box.

Mix the letters up in each word. Ask a friend to **solve** your word scramble and print the answers.

e.g. **upypp = puppy**

Word List

Scrambled Words	**Answers**
1. _____	_____
2. _____	_____
3. _____	_____
4. _____	_____
5. _____	_____
6. _____	_____
7. _____	_____
8. _____	_____
9. _____	_____
10. _____	_____

Name: _____

Title: _____

Author: _____

Vocabulary Development #8

Make a **word search** for a friend.

Choose **ten** words from your story. Print them **across**, **down** and **sideways**. Fill in the **spaces** with different letters.

List the words under the word search.

Word List:

_____ _____ _____

_____ _____ _____

Name: _____

Title: _____

Author: _____

Vocabulary Development #9

Find **ten** interesting words in your story.

e.g. | **fantastic, humungous, dinosaur, screech** |

Print a **list** of your words.

Share them with a friend.

Word List

1. _____   6. _____

2. _____   7. _____

3. _____   8. _____

4. _____   9. _____

5. _____   10. _____

Story Hamburger

Name: _____

Title: _____

Author: _____

Sequencing and Summarizing Events #1

Make a hamburger **summary** of your story.

Print **what happened** in each part of the story.

Beginning: _____
_____
_____

Middle: _____
_____
_____
_____
_____
_____

End: _____
_____
_____
_____

Sum It Up!

Name: _____

Title: _____

Author: _____

Sequencing and Summarizing Events #2

Sum up the **main things** that happened in your story.

Use the story to complete each sentence.

First _____

_____

Then _____

_____

Next _____

_____

After that _____

_____

In the end _____

_____

Comic Strip

Name: _____

Title: _____

Author: _____

Sequencing and Summarizing Events #3

Make a **comic strip** to tell your story.

eg.

1.	2.
3.	4.

News Report

Name: _____

Title: _____

Author: _____

Sequencing and Summarizing Events #4

Write a **news report** about what happened in your story.

Tell **who**, **what**, **where** and **when**.

e.g.

EXTRA!
The News
MORNING EDITION

_____

_____

_____

_____

_____

_____

_____

_____

Story Map

Name: _____

Title: _____

Author: _____

Sequencing and Summarizing Events #5

Draw a **map** to show where your story happens.

e.g.

Label your map with the names of the places in the story.

My Story Map

The Five W's

Name: _____

Title: _____

Author: _____

Sequencing and Summarizing Events #6

Sum up the story by writing the facts beside the **5 W's**.

Tell **how** these happened.

Who: _____

_____

What: _____

_____

Where: _____

_____

When: _____

_____

Why: _____

_____

How: _____

_____

Story Countdown

Name: _____

Title: _____

Author: _____

Sequencing and Summarizing Events #7

Think about the **most important things** that happened in the story.

List **ten** things in the order that they happened. Number each one like a countdown.

Number ten will be what happened at the **beginning** of the story. **Number one** will be something that happened at the **end** of the story.

10. _____

9. _____

8. _____

7. _____

6. _____

5. _____

4. _____

3. _____

2. _____

1. _____

Plot Line

Name: _____

Title: _____

Author: _____

Sequencing and Summarizing Events #8

Think about how the story began.

- What was the **first thing** that happened?

- What was the **most important action** in the story?

- How did the story **end**?

Use the **plot line** to print your answers?

_____

_____

The most important action in the story

_____

_____

The first thing that happened

_____

_____

How the story ended

Who, What, Where

Name: _____

Title: _____

Author: _____

Sequencing and Summarizing Events #9

Draw a picture of each **character** and print each characters's name.

Draw a picture of the **place** where the story happened.

Draw **two** pictures that show what **happened** in the story.

Print a **sentence** telling about your two pictures.

who	where
what #1 _____ _____	what #2 _____ _____

Character Web

Name: _____

Title: _____

Author: _____

Character Analysis #1

Choose a **character** from your story.

Draw a **web** with the character's name in the middle.

List **words** to describe your character around his or her name.

How does your character look, behave and feel?

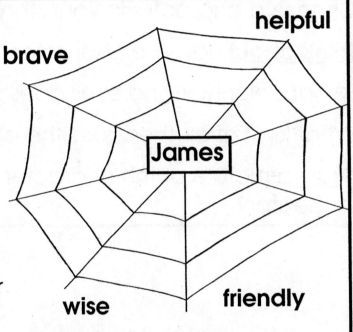

brave   helpful

James

wise   friendly

Character Portrait

Name: _____

Title: _____

Author: _____

Character Analysis #2

Choose a character in your story.

Think about how the character looks.

What color hair and eyes does the character have?

What kind of clothes does the character wear?

Draw a picture of this character. Show where he or she is in the story.

Clever Character

Name: _____

Title: _____

Author: _____

Character Analysis #3

Think of a character in the story.

Tell how the character showed that he or she was clever.

He or she was clever because.....

_____

_____

_____

_____

_____

_____

_____

Wanted Poster

Name: _____

Title: _____

Author: _____

Character Analysis #4

Choose one of the characters in your story.

Make a **Wanted Poster** that tells others what the character is wanted for, what he or she looks like, where he or she lives and the reward for finding the character.

Wanted!

Name: _____

Looks: _____

_____

_____

Last seen: _____

_____

Reward: _____

_____

Pen Pal

Name: _____

Title: _____

Author: _____

Character Analysis #5

Be a pen pal!

Write a **letter** to a character from your story.

What questions will you ask him or her?

Don't forget to tell the character all about yourself and what you like to do.

Dear _____ ,

_____

_____

_____

_____

_____

_____

Yours sincerely,

_____

Story Friend

Name: _____

Title: _____

Author: _____

Character Analysis #6

Choose a story character that you would like for a friend.

Tell what you and the story character would do together.

---

e.g. **I would like** _____ **for a friend. We would** _____ **together. Then we would go to** _____ **and** _____ .

I _____

_____

_____

_____

_____

_____

_____

Which Character?

Name: _____

Title: _____

Author: _____

Character Analysis #7

Which character would you like to be?

If you could be a character in the story, which one would you be?

Tell what you would do in the story.

e.g. **I would be James. If I were James I would ....**

_____

_____

_____

_____

_____

_____

_____

Design a T-Shirt

Name: _____

Title: _____

Author: _____

Creative Thinking #1

Design a T-shirt that will show others what your book is about.

Draw your design inside the shape of the T-shirt.

Make it **interesting** so that others will want to read your novel.

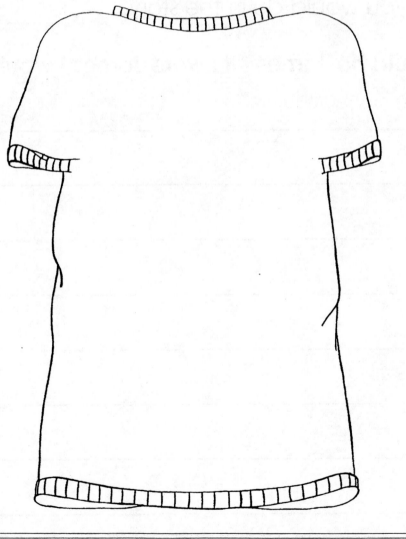

A New Book Cover

Name: _____

Title: _____

Author: _____

Creative Thinking #2

Design a new book cover for your story.

Print the **title** and **author** on the cover.

Which **picture** will you draw on the cover?

My Favorite Part

Name: _____

Title: _____

Author: _____

Creative Thinking #3

Draw a picture of your favorite part of the story.

Tell what is **happening** in your picture.

Design a Home

Name: _____

Title: _____

Author: _____

Creative Thinking #4

Design a home for your favorite character in the story.

What kind of home would he or she like?

Put Yourself in the Story

Name: _____

Title: _____

Author: _____

Creative Thinking #5

Make a picture of you in the story.

Be ready **to tell** us what you are doing in the picture.

Fact or Fiction?

Name: _____

Title: _____

Author: _____

Synthesis and Evaluation #1

Is the story a true story or did the author make it up?

Tell **four** things that make it true or not true.

TRUE   NO   FALSE
REAL   MAKE-   YES   BELIEVE

1. _____

_____

2. _____

_____

3. _____

_____

4. _____

_____

A Writer's Secrets

Name: _____

Title: _____

Author: _____

Synthesis and Evaluation #2

Find out the writer's secrets

If you met the author what might you ask him or her about story writing?

e.g. **I would like to know how you.........**

_____

_____

_____

_____

_____

_____

_____

A Story Frame

Name: _____

Title: _____

Author: _____

Synthesis and Evaluation #3

The problem begins when _____

_____

_____

_____

There is a problem because _____

_____

_____

_____

The problem is solved when_____

_____

_____

_____

Story Riddles

SSN1-165

Name: _____

Title: _____

Author: _____

Synthesis and Evaluation #4

Make up **two** riddles about the people, animals, places or things in your story.

Think of **three** clues for each riddle

e.g.

> **I have fur**
> **I live in the woods**
> **I met a girl with a red coat**
> **Who am I?**
>
> I am the big, bad wolf.

_____

_____

_____

_____

_____

_____

A New Ending

Name: _____

Title: _____

Author: _____

Synthesis and Evaluation #5

Make a **new** ending for the story.

You may want to **add** a new character.

e.g. | **The wolf and the three pigs lived happily together.** |

_____

_____

_____

_____

_____

_____

_____

_____

Good or Bad

Name: _____

Title: _____

Author: _____

Synthesis and Evaluation #6

Think of one character in the story.

Tell how you know that this character was good or bad.

e.g. | **Cinderella was good because she.......** |

_____

_____

_____

_____

_____

_____

_____

Like or Did Not Like

Name: _____

Title: _____

Author: _____

Synthesis and Evaluation #7

I liked ...., but I did not like.....

Write **two** sentences to tell what you liked about the story.

Write **two** sentences to tell what you did not like.

e.g.
| I liked the part when _____. |
| I did not like the way_____. |

1. _____

   _____

2. _____

   _____

1. _____

   _____

2. _____

   _____

Solve a Story Problem

Name: _____

Title: _____

Author: _____

Synthesis and Evaluation #8

Write about a problem one character
from your story had.

Tell how the problem was solved.

_____

_____

_____

_____

_____

_____

_____

_____

Story Feelings

Name: _____

Title: _____

Author: _____

Synthesis and Evaluation #9

Think about the different feelings in the story. How did it make you feel when you read it?

Look at the words below. **Think** about what happened in your story that was happy, sad, exciting, etc. Next to each word, **tell about** what happened.

happy: _____

sad: _____

exciting: _____

frightening: _____

funny: _____

strange: _____

wonderful: _____

52 SSN1-165

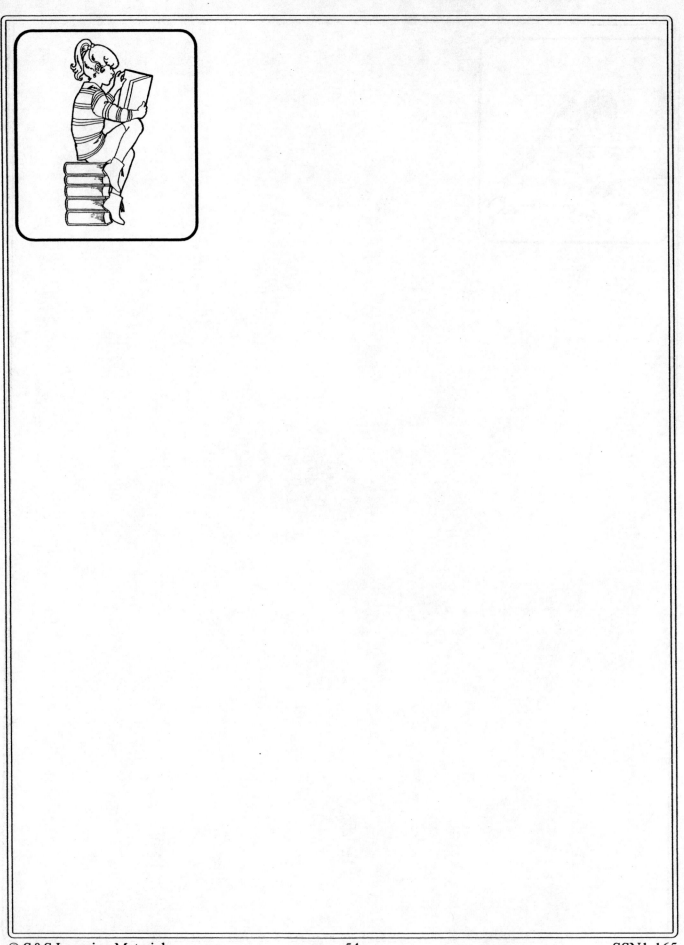